Deleted

ORIGAMI FUN

AIRCRAFT

BY ROBYN HARDYMAN
AND JESSICA MOON

BELLWETHER MEDIA • MINNEAPOLIS, MN

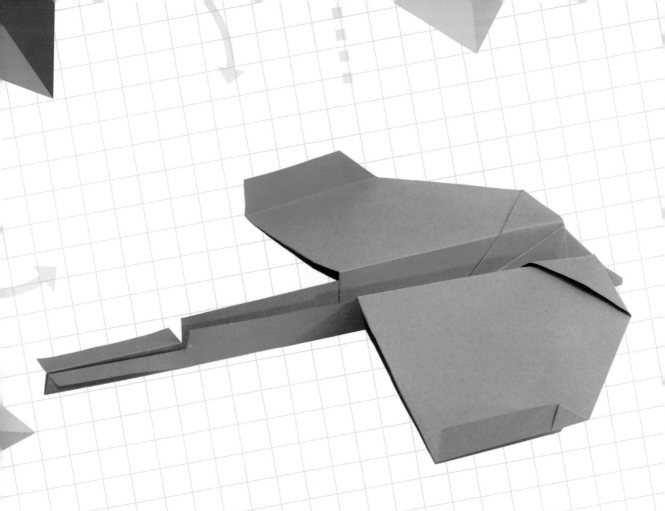

This edition first published in 2018 by Bellwether Media, Inc.

Library of Congress Cataloging-in-Publication Data

Names: Hardyman, Robyn, author.
Title: Aircraft / by Robyn Hardyman.
Description: Minneapolis, MN : Bellwether Media, Inc., 2018. | Series:
  Express! Origami Fun | Audience: Age 7-13. | Includes bibliographical
  references and index.
Identifiers: LCCN 2017000867 (print) | LCCN 2017003299 (ebook) | ISBN
  9781626177079 (hardcover : alk. paper) | ISBN 9781681034379 (ebook)
Subjects: LCSH: Origami–Juvenile literature. | Paper airplanes–Juvenile
  literature.
Classification: LCC TT872.5 .H37862 2018 (print) | LCC TT872.5 (ebook) | DDC
  736/.982–dc23
LC record available at https://lccn.loc.gov/2017000867

Editors: Sarah Eason and Harriet McGregor
Designers: Paul Myerscough and Jessica Moon

Printed in the United States of America, North Mankato, MN.

TABLE OF CONTENTS

ORIGAMI FUN

Origami is the art of folding paper. It has been used for hundreds of years. Origami artists make stunning animals, vehicles, and other models from a flat sheet of paper. They fold it carefully and slowly to create a work of art.

Anyone can learn the art of origami. In this book, you will learn how to make origami aircraft that really fly!

SUPPLIES
- colorful origami paper
- ruler or spoon for flattening folds
- scissors

ORIGAMI SYMBOLS

Below are key origami instruction symbols. You will find these throughout the book.

Valley fold	Mountain fold	Pleat fold	Cut line
Center line	Fold direction	Flip paper	Rotate paper

ORIGAMI FOLDS

Valley fold
Lift the paper and bend it toward you.

Mountain fold
Bend the paper backward, away from you.

Pleat fold
First fold the paper in one direction, and then fold it in the opposite direction.

Squash fold
Open two layers and squish them flat.

BASIC PLANE

Paper size:
Letter-size sheet of paper,
8.5 x 11 inches (21.6 x 27.9 centimeters)

This plane is really easy to put together. It is a great first origami to make. Take your time and be sure to make the creases sharp. To do this, press down firmly on each one.

1

Valley fold the bottom of the sheet to the top.

2

Valley fold the left corners into the center.

3

Mountain fold the top and bottom edges back.

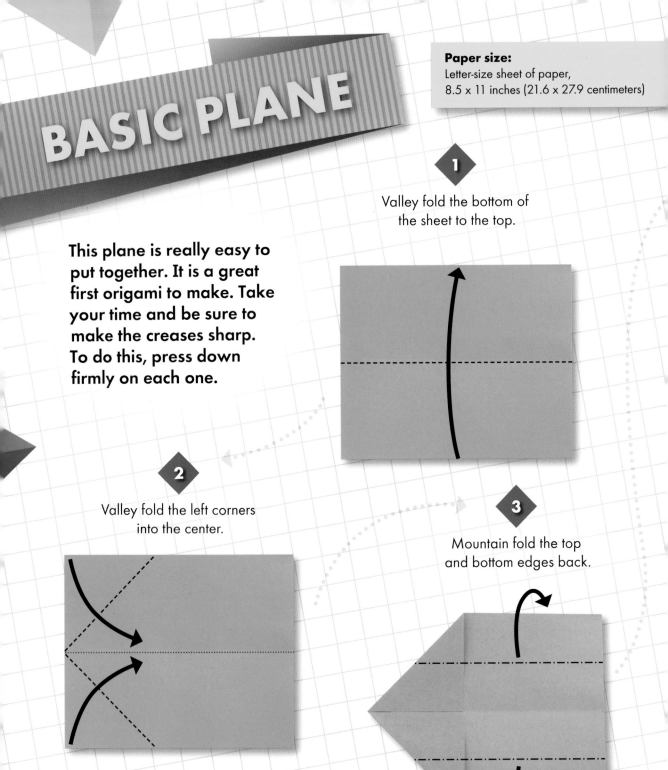

6

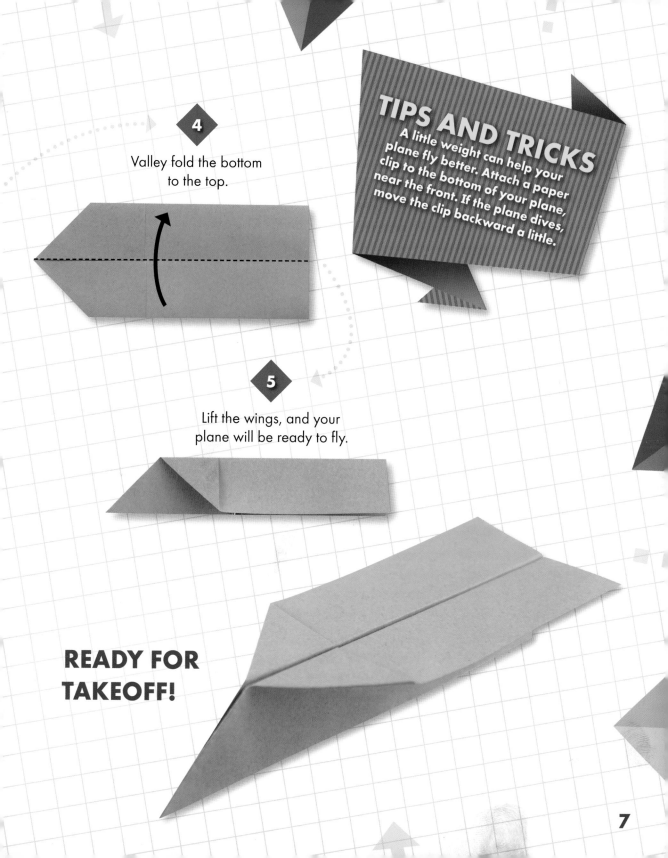

4

Valley fold the bottom to the top.

TIPS AND TRICKS

A little weight can help your plane fly better. Attach a paper clip to the bottom of your plane, near the front. If the plane dives, move the clip backward a little.

5

Lift the wings, and your plane will be ready to fly.

READY FOR TAKEOFF!

ARROW

Paper size:
Letter-size sheet of paper,
8.5 x 11 inches (21.6 x 27.9 centimeters)

Fold the sheet of paper in half, and then open it out. This marks the center line. Valley fold the top two corners down into the center.

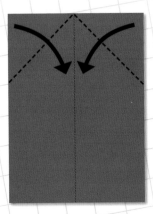

This plane looks simple and is easy to make. But you will be amazed how well it flies! The folded tip adds weight to the nose of the aircraft. This helps it soar straight and smooth.

Valley fold the left and right sides into the center.

Valley fold the nose of your plane down.

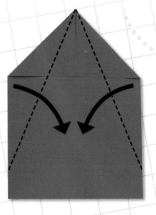

Your model should look like this. Now turn it over.

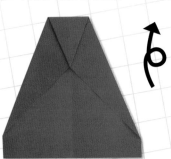

5

Valley fold the right side over to the left.

TIPS AND TRICKS
Origami is a calm hobby. Go slowly, and enjoy seeing your aircraft take shape.

6

Next, valley fold the upper left side over to the right. This creates the first wing.

7

Mountain fold the lower left side back. This creates the second wing. Your shooting arrow is ready for takeoff.

SUPER SHARP SOARER!

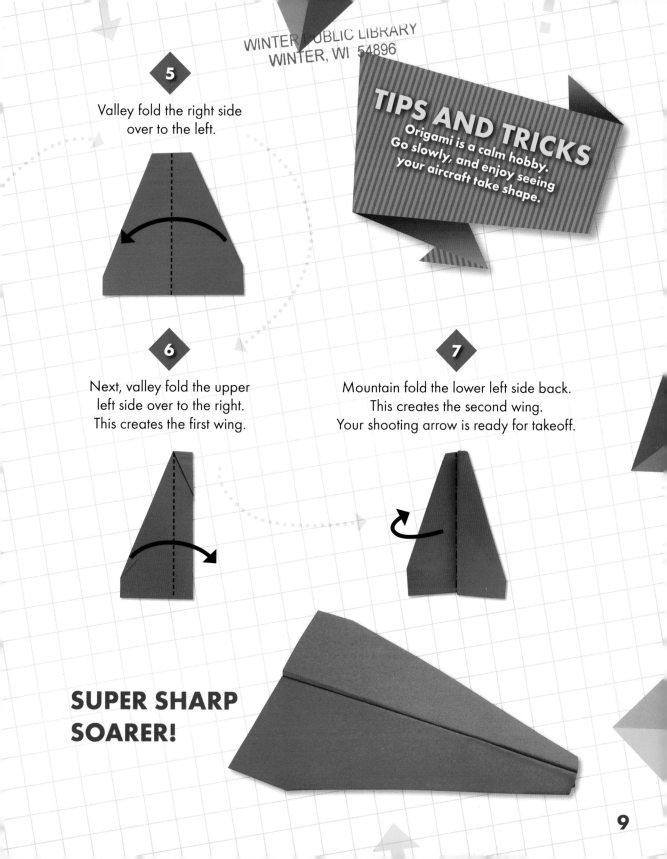

DART

Paper size:
Letter-size sheet of paper,
8.5 x 11 inches (21.6 x 27.9 centimeters)

This is another simple plane. But it is awesome, too! It is **streamlined** and sleek like a dart, so it can hit a target perfectly. Be careful making the first folds. Try to get a sharp point at the front.

Fold the sheet of paper in half, and then open it out. This marks the center line. Valley fold the left corners into the center.

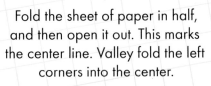

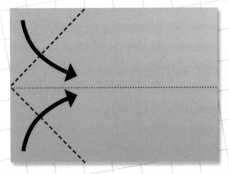

Valley fold the left top and bottom edges into the center.

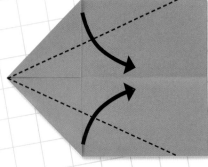

Valley fold the bottom up to the top.

4

Valley fold the top upper layer down. This makes a wide wing and a narrow body.

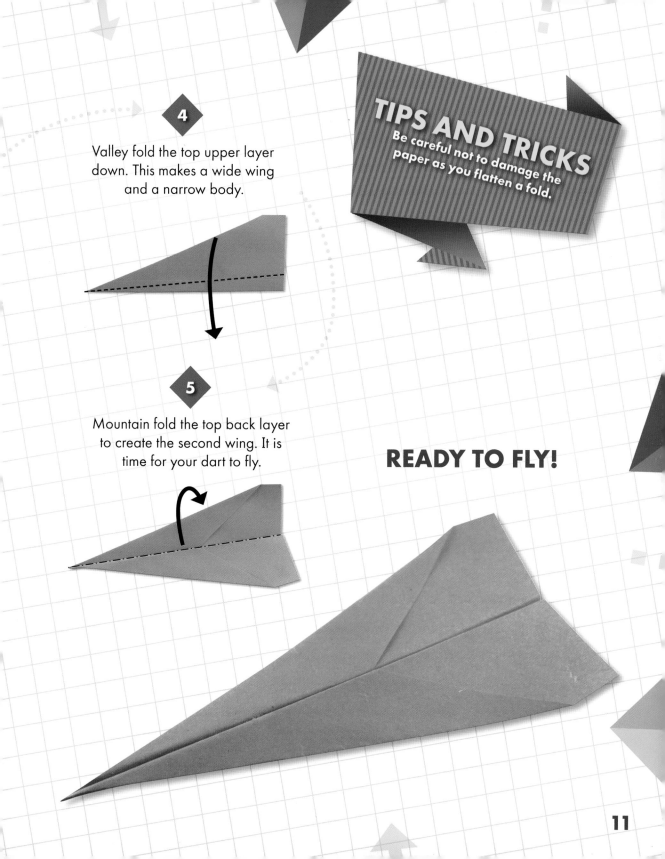

TIPS AND TRICKS
Be careful not to damage the paper as you flatten a fold.

5

Mountain fold the top back layer to create the second wing. It is time for your dart to fly.

READY TO FLY!

BULLET

Paper size:
Letter-size sheet of paper,
8.5 x 11 inches (21.6 x 27.9 centimeters)

This plane is like a military **jet**—sleek, very fast, and beautiful to look at. It is a little more difficult to make. But look at how it flies! It is sure to travel a long, long way!

Fold the sheet of paper in half, and then open it out. This marks the center line. Valley fold the left corners into the center.

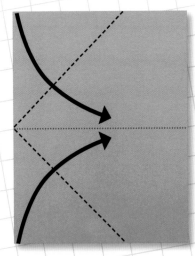

2

Valley fold the top and bottom edges into the center.

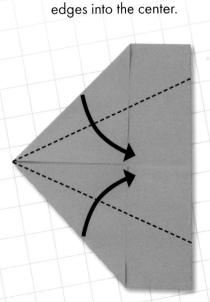

3

Next, valley fold the top and bottom edges into the center again.

4

Take the narrow nose of the aircraft, and valley fold it over to the right.

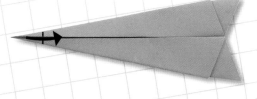

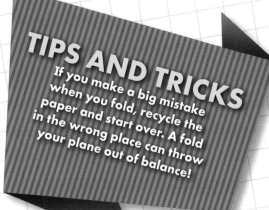

TIPS AND TRICKS

If you make a big mistake when you fold, recycle the paper and start over. A fold in the wrong place can throw your plane out of balance!

5

Valley fold the bottom edge up to the top.

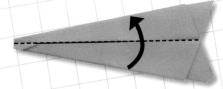

6

To create the first wing, valley fold the top upper layer down.

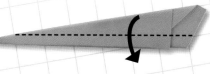

7

To create the second wing, mountain fold the top back layer. Your bullet plane is all set.

FAST AS A BULLET!

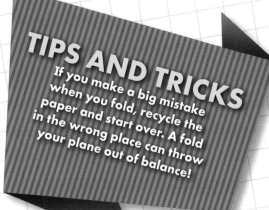

DELTA

Paper size:
Letter-size sheet of paper,
8.5 x 11 inches (21.6 x 27.9 centimeters)

This airplane can fly fast and completely straight. It has little winglets that turn up on the edges. These help to keep it **stable** in the air. The project is very easy to fold, too.

Fold the sheet of paper in half, and then open it out. This marks the center line. Valley fold the left corners into the center.

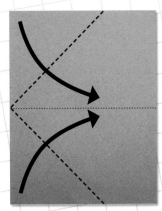

Valley fold the top and bottom edges into the center.

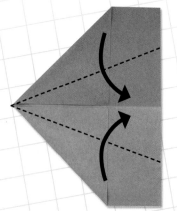

3

Take the nose of the plane, and valley fold it over to the right.

4

Valley fold the bottom edge up to the top.

To make the first wing, valley fold the top upper layer down.

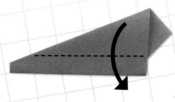

TIPS AND TRICKS

Make a soft crease in the paper. Make sure it's in the right place before you press down hard to make a sharp crease.

To make the winglets, valley fold the edges of each wing. To finish the second wing, mountain fold the top back layer.

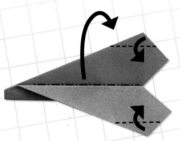

Open the wings a little, and your delta is ready for takeoff.

FAST FLIER!

SWALLOW

Paper size:
Letter-size sheet of paper,
8.5 x 11 inches (21.6 x 27.9 centimeters)

The swallow is an excellent flier. Some people think it is the best paper airplane there is! With its long tail, it looks like a bird in flight.

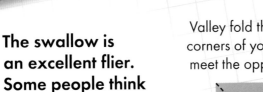

1

Valley fold the top left and right corners of your sheet of paper to meet the opposite edge. Unfold.

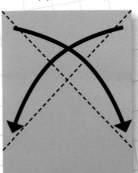

2

Valley fold the top down, and then unfold.

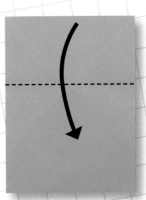

3

Push inward on the two side triangles. This will make a squash fold.

4

Take the upper left and right corners. Valley fold them to the top.

5

Valley fold the upper top layers down.

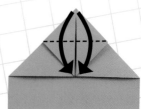

16

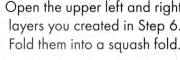

6

Valley fold the upper left and right layers into the center.

7

Open the upper left and right layers you created in Step 6. Fold them into a squash fold.

SQUASH FOLD   **SQUASH FOLD**

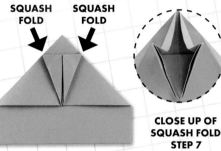

CLOSE UP OF SQUASH FOLD STEP 7

8

Mountain fold the top back layer behind your model. Cut off and keep the bottom section of your model.

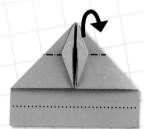

9

Mountain fold the left side of your model back. Then fold and cut the leftover section into a tail.

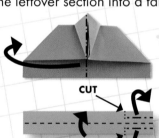

CUT

CUT

10

To make a wing, valley fold the upper right layer to the left.

11

To make a second wing, mountain fold the lower back layer behind your model.

12

Put the tail piece into the underside of the model. Push it as far as it will go.

13

Turn the model over, and then launch your swallow.

ZOOOOM!

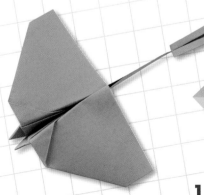

CONDOR

The flight path of this plane is slow and very smooth. Launch it across the room. Then watch it glide like a **condor**, the huge, soaring bird! The winglets help keep it stable in the air and fly straight.

Paper size:
Letter-size sheet of paper,
8.5 x 11 inches (21.6 x 27.9 centimeters)

1

Fold the sheet of paper in half, and then open it out. This marks the center line. Valley fold the top left and right corners into the center.

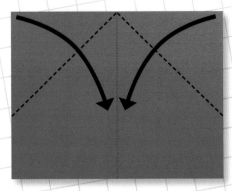

2

Take the aircraft's nose, and valley fold it down.

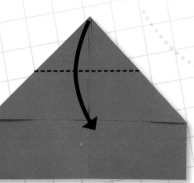

3

Valley fold the top left and right edges toward the center.

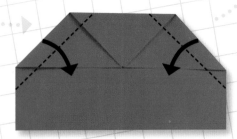

4

Pleat fold the center to create your condor's body. To do this, make the central fold a valley fold. The two folds on either side are mountain folds.

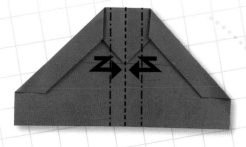

TIPS AND TRICKS

When you launch this one, do not throw it too hard. It will fly better this way.

5

Fold up the left and right wing edges. Your condor is now ready to take flight.

SOARS LIKE A BIRD!

19

GLIDER

Paper size:
Square sheet of origami paper,
6 x 6 inches (15 x 15 centimeters)

Have you ever seen a circular plane? Maybe not, but this **glider** really does fly! Use a square sheet of paper this time. The glider does not need to be thrown to launch. Just drop it from a height and watch it go.

Valley fold the bottom corner of your sheet of paper to the top corner.

Take a small section at the bottom, and valley fold it up.

Curve the left and right edges toward one another.

20

4

Slot the left side into the right.

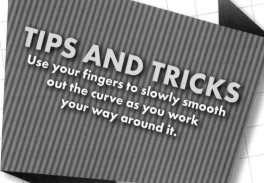

TIPS AND TRICKS
Use your fingers to slowly smooth out the curve as you work your way around it.

5

Your glider should now look like this. Hold it above your head by the pointed part. Let go of the glider, and it will glide gently down.

WATCH IT GLIDE!

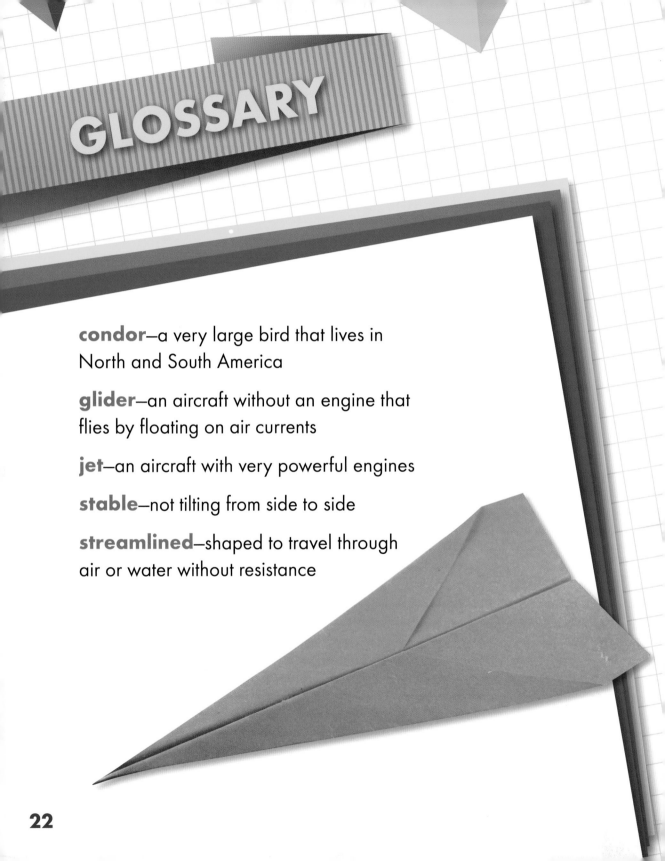

GLOSSARY

condor—a very large bird that lives in North and South America

glider—an aircraft without an engine that flies by floating on air currents

jet—an aircraft with very powerful engines

stable—not tilting from side to side

streamlined—shaped to travel through air or water without resistance

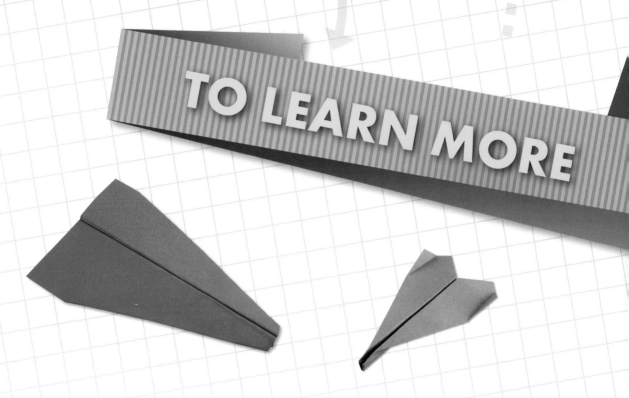

TO LEARN MORE

AT THE LIBRARY

Dewar, Andrew. *Ultimate Paper Airplanes for Kids: The Best Guide to Paper Airplanes.* North Clarendon, Vt.: Tuttle Publishing, 2015.

Nahum, Andrew. *Flight.* New York, N.Y.: DK Pub., 2011.

Naylor, Amy. *Whoosh! Easy Paper Airplanes for Kids: Color, Fold, and Fly!* Mineola, N.Y.: Dover Publications, 2013.

ON THE WEB

Learning more about aircraft origami is as easy as 1, 2, 3.

1. Go to www.factsurfer.com.

2. Enter "aircraft origami" into the search box.

3. Click the "Surf" button, and you will see a list of related web sites.

With factsurfer.com, finding more information is just a click away.

INDEX

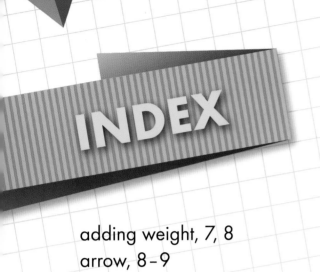